SINGERS & SONGWRITERS

An outstanding collection of thirty-two songs from five of this generation's most influential musical artists. Arranged for piano/vocal with chord diagrams and full lyrics.

AMSCO PUBLICATIONS
NEW YORK/LONDON/SYDNEY

Photo of Leonard Cohen by Dominique Isserman
Photo of Judy Collins courtesy of Judy Collins
Photo of Bob Dylan by Ken Regan/Camera 5
Photo of Paul Simon courtesy of Paul Simon
Photo of Cat Stevens by Michael Putland/Retna Ltd.

Order No. AM 85580
International Standard Book Number: 0.8256.1320.5

Exclusive Distributors:
Music Sales Corporation
257 Park Avenue South, New York, NY 10010
Music Sales Limited
8/9 Frith Street, London W1V 5TZ England
Music Sales Pty. Limited
120 Rothschild Street, Rosebery, Sydney, NSW 2018, Australia

Printed in the United States of America by
Vicks Lithograph and Printing Corporation

Suzanne

Words and Music by Leonard Cohen

Bm/F♯
F♯m
E
spend the night be - side her. And you know that she's half
A/E
E
cra - zy, but that's why you want to be there. And she
G♯m
C♯m/G♯
A
feeds you tea and or - ang - es that come all the way from
D/A
Chi - na. And just when you mean to tell her that you

F♯m
Bm/F♯
F♯m
E
have no love to give her, Then she gets you on her
A/E
E
F♯m
Bm/F♯
F♯m
wave - length, And she lets the riv - er an - swer that you've al -
E
A/E
ways been her lov - er.
G♯m
4fr.
C♯m/G♯
4fr.
G♯m
4fr.
And you want to trav - el with her, And you

A D/A A E

want to trav - el blind. And you know she will trust

A/E E F♯m

you, for you've touched her per - fect bod - y with your

1., 2.
E

mind.

2. And
3. Now Suz -

3.
E A/E E

mind.

ritard.

Additional Lyrics

2. And Jesus was a sailor
When he walked upon the water,
And he spent a long time watching
From his lonely wooden tower.
And when he knew for certain
Only drowning men could see him,
He said,"All men will be sailors then
Until the sea shall free them."
But he himself was broken,
Long before the sky would open.
Forsaken, almost human,
He sank beneath your wisdom like a stone.
And you want to travel with him,
And you want to travel blind,
And you think maybe you'll trust him,
For he's touched your perfect body
with his mind.

3. Now Suzanne takes your hand,
And she leads you to the river.
She is wearing rags and feathers
From Salvation Army counters.
And the sun pours down like honey
On our lady of the harbour.
And she shows you where to look
Among the garbage and the flowers.
There are heroes in the seaweed,
There are children in the morning,
They are leaning out for love,
And they will lean that way forever.
While Suzanne holds the mirror.
And you want to travel with her,
And you want to travel blind,
And you know that you can trust her,
For she's touched your perfect body
with her mind.

Bird On A Wire

Words and Music by Leonard Cohen

G
D
If I, if I have been un - kind,
Em
D
I hope that you can just let it go by.
G
D
If I, if I have been un - true,
Em
A
I hope you know it was nev - er to you.
More like a

D
A
D
G
ba - by still - born, like a beast with his horn, I have
D
A
D
torn ev - 'ry - one who reached out for me.
D
A
D
But I swear by this song, and by all that I have done
G
D
A
D
wrong, I will make it all up to thee.

G
I saw a beg - gar lean - ing on his wood - en
D
crutch.
Em
He said to me,
D
"You must not ask for so much."
G
3
3
And a pret - ty wom - an lean - ing in her dark - ened door,
D

Em
She cried to me, "Hey, why not ask for
A
more?"
More like a bird
D
on the
A
wire,
like a drunk
D
in a mid-night
G
choir, I have
D
tried in my
A
way to be
G
free.
D
ritard.

Hey That's No Way To Say Goodbye

Words and Music by Leonard Cohen

Bb
know that we are not new, In cit - y and in for - est, they
Gm
smiled like me and you. But now it's come to dis - tanc - es and
Eb
both of us must try. Your eyes are soft with sor - row.
F
Hey, that's no way to say good -

Additional Lyrics

2. I'm not looking for another
As I wander in my time.
Walk me to the corner,
Our steps will always rhyme.
You know my love goes with you
As your love stays with me,
It's just the way it changes
Like the shoreline and the sea.
But let's not talk of love or chains
And things we can't untie,
Your eyes are soft with sorrow,
Hey, that's no way to say goodbye.

3. I loved you in the morning,
Our kisses deep and warm,
Your hair upon the pillow,
Like a sleepy golden storm.
Yes, many loved before us,
I know that we are not new,
In city and in forest,
They smiled like me and you.
But let's not talk of love or chains
And things we can't untie,
Your eyes are soft with sorrow,
Hey, that's no way to say goodbye.

I'm Your Man

Words and Music by Leonard Cohen

D
No chord
Em
ask me to. And if you want an - oth - er kind of love,
D
No chord
I'll wear a mask for you. If you want a
Bm
G
part - ner, take my hand, or if you want to strike me down in
Bm
A
No chord
an - ger, here I stand. I'm your

Bm
No chord
Em
man.
If you want a box - er, I will
D
No chord
step in - to the ring for you.
And if you want a
Em
D
doc - tor, I'll ex - am - ine ev - 'ry inch of you.
No chord
Bm
If you want a driv - er, climb in - side.
Or if you want to

G
Bm
A
take me for a ride, You know you can.
No chord
Bm
I'm your man. Ah, the
D
G
A
moon's too bright, the chain's too tight, the beast won't go to sleep.
D
F♯m
I've been run-ning through these prom-is-es to you that I

Bm
F♯
made and I could not keep.
Ah, but a man nev - er got a
Bm
wom - an back, not by beg - ging on his knees.
Or I'd
G
F♯
crawl to you, ba - by, and I'd fall at your feet, and I'd
G
F♯
howl at your beau - ty like a dog in heat. And I'd

G
E
claw at your heart, and I'd tear at your sheet. I'd say, please,
A
Bm
please, I'm your man.
No chord
Em
And if you've got to sleep for a mo - ment
D
No chord
on the road, I will steer for you.
And if you want to

Em
D
work the street a - lone, I'll dis - ap - pear for you.
No chord
Bm
If you want a fa - ther for your child, or on - ly want to
G
A
walk with me a - while a - cross the sand,
No chord
Bm
A
Bm
I'm your man.

So Long, Marianne

Words and Music by Leonard Cohen

Moderately slow, in 2

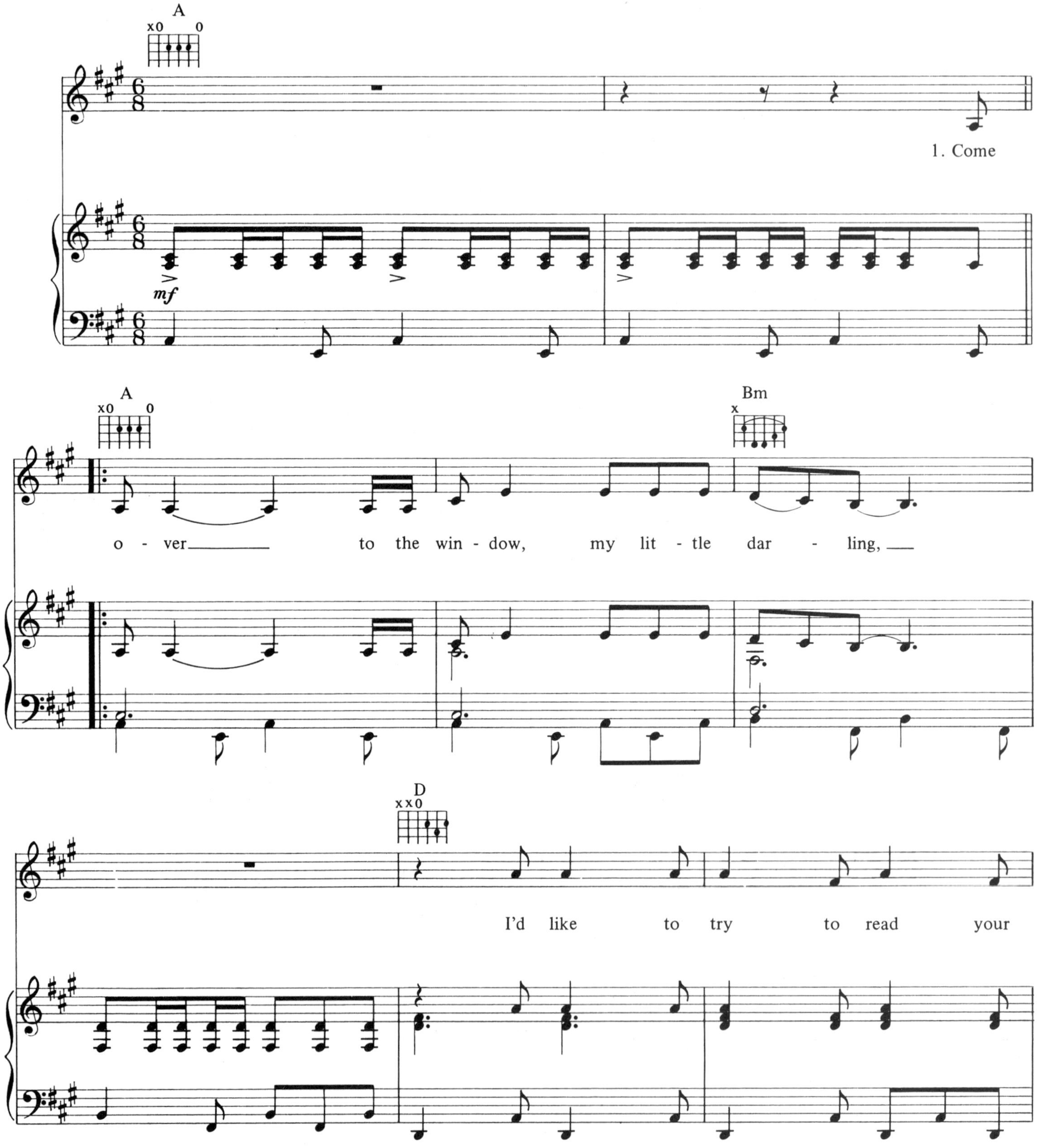

A

1. Come

A Bm

o - ver to the win - dow, my lit - tle dar - ling,

D

I'd like to try to read your

A
G
palm.
I used to think
D
I was some_ sort of gyp - sy boy
F♯m
E
Esus4
Be - fore I let you take me home.
E
E7
Chorus:
A
Now, so long, Ma - ri - anne,

F♯m
E
Esus4
It's time that we be - gan_ to laugh and
E
E7
E
Esus4
E
E7
cry and cry and laugh a - bout it
A
Asus4
A
all a - gain.
Asus4
1.- 6.
A
7.
A
2. Well,

Additional Lyrics

2. Well, you know that I love to live with you,
   But you make me forget so very much.
   I forget to pray for the angel,
   And then the angels forget to pray for us.
   Chorus

3. We met when we were almost young,
   Deep in the green lilac park.
   You held on to me like I was a crucifix,
   As we went kneeling through the dark.
   Chorus

4. Your letters, they all say that you're beside me now.
   Then why do I feel alone?
   I'm standing on a ledge, and your fine spider web
   Is fastening my ankle to a stone.
   Chorus

5. For now I need your hidden love,
   I'm cold as a new razor blade.
   You left when I told you I was curious,
   I never said that I was brave.
   Chorus

6. Oh, you're really such a pretty one.
   I see you've gone and changed your name again,
   And just when I climbed this whole mountainside
   To wash my eyelids in the rain.
   Chorus

7. O your eyes, well, I forget your eyes,
   Your body's at home in every sea.
   How come you gave away your news to everyone,
   That you said was a secret for me?
   Chorus

First We Take Manhattan

Words and Music by Leonard Cohen

Dm
I'm com - ing now, I'm com - ing to re -
I'm guid - ed by the beau - ty of our
Am
ward them.
weap - ons.
G
First we take Man -
F
Esus4
E
hat - tan, then we take Ber -
Am
1.
lin.
I'm

2.
C
F/C
C
I'd real - ly like to live be - side you,
G
F
F/G
G
C
ba - by.
I love your bod - y and your
F/C
C
Am
Asus2
Am
spir - it and your clothes.
But you
C
Csus4
C
Dm/A
Am
see that line there mov - ing through the sta - tion?

G
F
And I told you, and I told you, I
Esus4
E
Am
told you I was one of those.
Ah, you
Dm
Am
loved me as a los - er, but now you're wor - ried that I just might win.
Dm
You know the way to stop me, but you

Am Dm

don't have the dis - ci - pline. How man - y nights I

Am

prayed for this: to let my work be - gin.

G G/F G E7sus4 E *To Coda*

First we take Man - hat - tan, then we take Ber -

Am *D.S. (to 2nd ending) al Coda*

lin.

Coda
Am
G/A
lin.
F/A
E7sus4
Ah, re -
Dm
mem - ber me,
I used to live for
Am
Dm
mu - sic,
And re - mem-ber me,

Am
I brought your gro - ceries in.
Well, it's
Dm
Fa - ther's Day
and ev - ery - bod - y's
Am
wound - ed.
G
First we take Man -
(melody)
Dm6/F
E7sus4
E
hat - tan,
then we take Ber -
(melody)

Additional Lyrics

From D.S.
I don't like your fashion business, mister.
I don't like these drugs that keep you thin.
I don't like what happened to my sister.
First we take Manhattan, then we take Berlin.

(Bridge):
I'd really like to live beside you, baby.
I love your body and your spirit and your clothes.
But you see that line there moving through the station?
And I told you, and I told you,
I told you I was one of those,

And I thank you for those items that you sent me:
The monkey and the plywood violin.
I practiced every night and now I'm ready.
First we take Manhattan, then we take Berlin. *(To Coda)*

Famous Blue Raincoat

Words and Music by Leonard Cohen

Cm
Dm
I'm writ - ing you now just to see if you're bet - ter.
Gm
E♭
New York is cold, but I like where I'm liv - ing, The
Cm
Dm
mus - ic on Clin - ton Street all through the eve - ning.
Gm
Am7
I hear that you're build - ing your lit - tle

Gm7
Am7
house deep in the des - ert.
Gm7
F
You're liv - ing for noth - ing now. I hope you're
Gm7
F
Chorus:
keep - ing some kind of rec - ord. Yes, 'n
B♭
Jane came by with a lock of your

F
hair, She said that you gave it to
Gm7
her that night that you planned to go
Am7
F
To Coda
clear.
And)
Eb
Dm7
1.
2.
Did you ev - er go clear?
2. The
poco rit.
poco rit.

Gm
Eb
a tempo
Cm
Cm7
Dm7
D.S. al Coda
3. And
poco rit.
Coda
Bb
F
Jane came by with a lock of your hair,
Gm7
She said that you gave it to her that

Additional Lyrics

2. The last time we saw you, you looked so much older,
Your famous blue raincoat was torn at the shoulder.
You'd been to the station to meet ev'ry train,
You came home without Lili Marlene.
And you treated my woman to a flake of your life,
And when she came back, she was nobody's wife.

Chorus: Well, I see you there with a rose in your teeth, one more thin gypsy thief.
Well, I see Jane's away, she sends her regards.

3. And what can I tell you my brother, my killer,
What can I possibly say?
I guess that I miss you, I guess I forgive you,
I'm glad you stood in my way.
If you ever come by here for Jane or for me,
Well, your enemy is sleeping and his woman is free.

Chorus: Yes, thanks for the trouble you took from her eyes.
I thought it was there for good, so I never tried.

Coda: And Jane came by with a lock of your hair,
She said that you gave it to her,
That night that you planned to go clear.
Sincerely, L. Cohen.

Amazing Grace

Words and Music by John Newton
Arranged and Adapted by Judy Collins

E
A
E
3. man - y dan - gers, toils and snares we
4. we've been there ten thou - sand years, bright
B
B7
E
have al rea - dy come. 'Twas grace that
shi - ning as the sun. We've no less
E7
A
E
B6
B7
brought us safe thus far, and grace will lead us
days to sing God's praise than when we first be -
E
After 2nd time
D.S. al Coda
Coda
A6
E
home. 4. When
gun. 1. A -
see.
ritard. e dim.

Hard Time For Lovers

Words and Music by Hugh Prestwood

B♭/F
F
Fmaj7
B♭/F
F
Verse:
B♭/F
B♭/C
F
2. Talk - in' on the phone to Kirk — to - day, He said that he and Liz were through —
Gm7
B♭/C
F
Gm7
And by the way that things have been go - in', — You can
B♭
Dm
Am
say that they were o - ver - due, — For ev - 'ry oth - er mar - ried pair —

Dm
Am
Dm
of us they'd al - read - y split in two.
Gm7
B♭6
B♭maj7
Dm
Each of us turn - in' out our lights a - lone, or sleep - in' with some - one
B♭/C
Chorus:
F
Fmaj7
new, ain't it true. These are hard times for lov -
f
Gm7
B♭/C
Dm
F/C
Gm7
B♭/C
ers, Ev - 'ry - one wants to be free. Ain't these

F
Fmaj7
Gm7
B♭/C
Dm
F/C
hard times for lov - ers, Ev - 'ry-one's sing-in', "I
B♭
Dm
C
B♭
B♭/C
F
Fmaj7
got-ta be me with-out you."
B♭/F
F
Fmaj7
B♭/F
To next strain
Fine
B♭/C
F
Verse:
3. Now
rall.
F
B♭/F
B♭/C
F
Gm7
B♭/C
hon-ey, I'm sup-posed to tell you I've got to live for to-day. And
mf

F
Gm7
B♭
don't you know it is my life - time, I've got to live it my own way.
Dm
Am
Dm
Am
But late-ly I can't help think-in' I reap what I
Dm
Gm7
B♭6
B♭ maj7
sow. For all of my ho - ly free - dom,
Dm
B♭/C
D.S. al Fine
what have I got to show? I don't know! These are

Cook With Honey

Words and Music by Valerie Carter

D
G/A
D
sweet-en up the night.
We al - ways
cook with hon -
G/A
D
G/A
ey, Tell me how's your ap - pe - tite
for some sweet
D
G/A
D
To Coda
G/A
Verse:
love?
2. Find - in'
D
G/A
D
fav - or with your neigh - bor,
Well, it can be so

G/A
D
fine, It's eas - i - er than pie to be kind.
We've been search - ing for so long,
Now our house is
turned in to a home.
Chorus:
D.S. al Coda
'Cause I al - ways
Coda
Verse:
3. Well, our

D
G/A
door is al - ways o - pen, And there's
come and get to know us, There'll be a
D
G/A
D
sure - ly room for more. Cook - in' where there's
place set just for you. Sweet wine be - fore
G/A
D
G/A
good love Is nev - er an - y chore.
din - ner, That is sure - ly bound to soothe.
1.
D
G/A
2.
Chorus:
4. So I al - ways

D
G/A
D
cook with hon - ey To sweet - en up the night.
G/A
D
G/A
We al - ways cook with hon - ey, Tell me
D
G/A
D
how's your ap - pe - fite for some sweet love.
A
D
A
G/A
Repeat and fade
I al - ways

Trust Your Heart

Words and Music by Judy Collins

Gm6/D
D
In their light
Some we keep
Gm6/D
D
our voic - es trem - ble with re - flect - ions
to light the dark nights on a jour - ney
Em6/C♯
Bm
D/A
G6
G/A
Of what we know and what we leave to
And shine be - yond the days when we have
Em7
Bm
F♯m/A
chance. The heart can see be -
loved. The heart can see be -

Em7
G
Em7/A
A7
yond the sun.
yond our prayers.
Be - yond the turn - ing
Be - yond our fond - est
Bm
Gm6/D
D
moon.
schemes.
And as we look, the
And tell us which are
1. A/G
G
D/A
Em7
heart will teach us all we need to
C
A7♭9
learn.
poco rit.

2.
A/G
G
D/A
Em7
made for fools, and
C
A7♭9
which are wise men's dreams.
poco rit.
D
Trust your heart,
mp freely
Gm6/D
D
Trust your heart.
ritard. e dim.
R.H.
pp

Since You've Asked

Words and Music by Judy Collins

Am7
D9
Am7
D9
Take the roads that I have walked a - long, look-ing for to - mor - row's
B
Gsus2
Em
time. . . peace of mind. As my life spills in - to
poco rit.
a tempo
Bsus4
G
Asus4
A
Em
yours. chang - ing with the hours; Fill - ing up the world with
Bsus4
G
Asus4
A
Am7
time. turn - ing time to flow - ers; I can show you all the

D9
Am7
D9
B
Gsus2
songs that I nev - er sang to one man be - fore.
poco rit.
G
A7sus4
A7sus4
A
We have seen a mil - lion stones ly - ing by the wa - ter.
a tempo
G
A7sus4
A
You have climbed the hills with me to the moun - tain shel - ter,
Am7
C/D
Am7
Tak - en off the days one by one, Set - ting them to breathe in the

Fmaj7
Esus4
Em
sun.
Take the lil - ies and the
poco rit.
a tempo
Bsus4
G
Asus4
A
Em
lace
from the days
of
child - hood,
All the wil - low wind - ing
Bsus4
G
Asus4
A
Am7
D9
paths
lead - ing up
and
out - ward,
This is what I give,
Am7
D9
B
Gsus2
G
This is what I ask
you
for,
noth - ing more.
poco a poco ritard.

My Father

Words and Music by Judy Collins

Moderately, in 6, nostalgic

D
Bm7
Esus4
E
F♯m
A/E
E♭
Cm7
Fsus4
F
Gm
B♭/F
and I would learn to dance. We lived in O-
B7
E
G♯m/D♯
4fr.
C♯m
4fr.
E/B
C7
F
Am/E
Dm
F/C
hi-o then; he worked in the mines.
Em
G/D
A7/C♯
A7
D
Fm
A♭/E♭
B♭7/D
B♭7
E♭
On his streams like boats we knew we'd sail

Verse 2. All my sisters soon were gone
to Denver and Cheyenne,
Marrying their grownup dreams,
the lilacs and the man.
I stayed behind the youngest still,
only danced alone,
The colors of my father's dreams
faded without a sigh.

3. And I live in Paris now,
my children dance and dream
Hearing the ways of a miner's life
in words they've never seen.
I sail my memories of home
like boats across the Seine,
And watch the Paris sun
set in my father's eyes again.

4. My father always promised us
that we would live in France.
We'd go boating on the Seine
and I would learn to dance.
I sail my memories afar
like boats across the Seine,
And watch the Paris sun
set in my father's eyes again.

Blowin' In The Wind

Words and Music by Bob Dylan

G A D
seas must a white dove sail be - fore she
ears must one - man have be - fore he can
G A D
sleeps in the sand? Yes, 'n' how man - y
hear peo - ple cry? Yes, 'n' how man - y
G A D
times must the can - non - balls fly be - fore they're
deaths will it take 'til he knows and that too man - y
G D G
for - ev - er banned?
peo ple have died?
The an - swer, my

Additional Lyrics

3. How many years can a mountain exist
before it is washed to the sea?
Yes 'n' how many years can some people exist
before they're allowed to be free?
Yes 'n' how many times can a man turn his head
pretending that he just doesn't see?

The answer, my friend, is blowin' in the wind,
The answer is blowin' in the wind.

I Shall Be Released

Words and Music by Bob Dylan

Bm
C♯m
4fr.
flec - tion
Some place
E9sus4
A
D/A
A
so high a - bove the wall.
Chorus:
Bm
I see my light come shin - ing
C♯m
4fr.
E9sus4
From the west down to the

Additional Lyrics

2. Down here next to me in this lonely crowd
   Is a man who swears he's not to blame.
   All day long I hear him cry so loud,
   Calling out that he's been framed.

   Chorus

3. They say ev'rything can be replaced,
   Yet ev'ry distance is not near.
   So I remember ev'ry face
   Of ev'ry man who put me here.

   Chorus

Forever Young

Words and Music by Bob Dylan

G D G C
stay for - ev - er young, May you
G D G
stay for - ev - er young. 2. May you
C G
grow up to be right - eous, May you grow up to be true. May you
hands al - ways be bus - y, May your feet al - ways be swift. May you
D
al - ways know the truth, And see the lights sur - round - ing you. May you
have a strong foun - da - tion when the winds of chang - es shift. May your

G
C
al - ways be cou - ra - geous, Stand up - right and be strong.
heart al - ways be joy - ful, May your song al - ways be sung.
May you
May you
1.
G
D
G
C
stay for - ev - er young,
May you
G
D
G
stay for - ev - er young.
3. May you
2. G
D
stay for - ev - er
G
C
G
D
G
young,
May you stay for - ev - er young.

Tangled Up In Blue

Words and Music by Bob Dylan

D
C/D
red.
Her folks, they said our lives__ to-geth-er
Sure was gon-na be rough._
They nev-er did like__ Ma-ma's
G
home-made dress,_ Pa-pa's bank-book was-n't big e-nough.
And
A
Bm
I was stand-in' on the side of the road,_
Rain fall-in' on my shoes.__

G
A
Bm
Head - ing out for the East Coast, Lord
D
G
A
knows I've paid some dues Get - tin' through.
C
G
D
D sus4 sus2
Tan - gled up in blue.
1.-6.
D
D sus4 sus2
7.
C
G
D

Additional Lyrics

2. She was married when we first met,
Soon to be divorced.
I helped her out of a jam, I guess,
But I used a little too much force.
We drove that car as far as we could,
Abandoned it out West.
Split up on a dark sad night,
Both agreeing it was best.
She turned around to look at me,
As I was walkin' away.
I heard her say over my shoulder,
"We'll meet again some day
on the avenue."
Tangled up in blue.

3. I had a job in the great north woods,
Working as a cook for a spell.
But I never did like it all that much,
And one day the axe just fell.
So I drifted down to New Orleans,
Where I happened to be employed.
Workin' for a while on a fishin' boat,
Right outside of Delacroix.
But all the while I was alone,
The past was close behind.
I seen a lot of women,
But she never escaped my mind,
And I just grew.
Tangled up in blue.

4. She was workin' in a topless place,
And I stopped in for a beer.
I just kept lookin' at the side of her face,
In the spotlight so clear.
And later on as the crowd thinned out,
I's just about to do the same.
She was standing there in back of my chair,
Said to me, "Don't I know your name?"
I muttered somethin' underneath my breath,
She studied the lines on my face.
I must admit I felt a little uneasy,
When she bent down to tie the laces
Of my shoe.
Tangled up in blue.

5. She lit a burner on the stove,
And offered me a pipe.
"I thought you'd never say hello," she said,
"You look like the silent type."
Then she opened up a book of poems,
And handed it to me.
Written by an Italian poet
From the thirteenth century.
And every one of them words rang true,
And glowed like burnin' coal.
Pourin' off of every page,
Like it was written in my soul
From me to you.
Tangled up in blue.

6. I lived with them on Montague Street,
In a basement down the stairs.
There was music in the cafes at night,
And revolution in the air.
Then he started into dealing with slaves,
And something inside of him died.
She had to sell everything she owned,
And froze up inside.
And when finally the bottom fell out,
I became withdrawn.
The only thing I knew how to do,
Was to keep on keepin' on,
Like a bird that flew.
Tangled up in blue.

7. So now I'm goin' back again,
I got to get to her somehow.
All the people we used to know,
They're an illusion to me now.
Some are mathematicians,
Some are carpenters' wives.
Don't know how it all got started,
I don't know what they're doin' with their lives.
But me, I'm still on the road,
Headin' for another joint.
We always did feel the same,
We just saw it from a different point
Of view.
Tangled up in blue.

Knockin' On Heaven's Door

Words and Music by Bob Dylan

G
D
C
I feel like I'm knock-in' on heav-en's door.
I feel like I'm knock-in' on heav-en's door.
G
D
Am7
G
D
C
Knock, knock, knock-in' on heav-en's door,
Knock, knock, knock-in' on heav-en's door,
G
D
Am7
G
D
Knock, knock, knock-in' on heav-en's door,
Knock, knock, knock-in' on heav-en's door.
1. C
2. C
G
D
Am7
Repeat and fade
mp

Lay, Lady, Lay

Words and Music by Bob Dylan

E
F#m
A
5fr.
C#m/G#
4fr.
I'll show them to you and you'll see them shine.
Lay, la - dy, lay,
G
3fr.
Bm/F#
C#m
4fr.
Bm
lay a - cross my big brass bed.
Stay, la - dy, stay,
stay with your man a - while.
Un - til the break of day,
let me see you make him smile.

E
F♯m
A
5fr.
His clothes are dirt - y but his
hands are clean,
E
F♯m
A
5fr.
And you're the best thing that he's
ev - er seen.
C♯m/G♯
4fr.
G
3fr.
Bm/F♯
A
5fr.
C♯m
4fr.
Stay, la - dy, stay,
stay with your man a - while.
G
3fr.
Bm
C♯m
4fr.
E
F♯m
A
5fr.
Why wait an - y long - er for the world to be - gin,

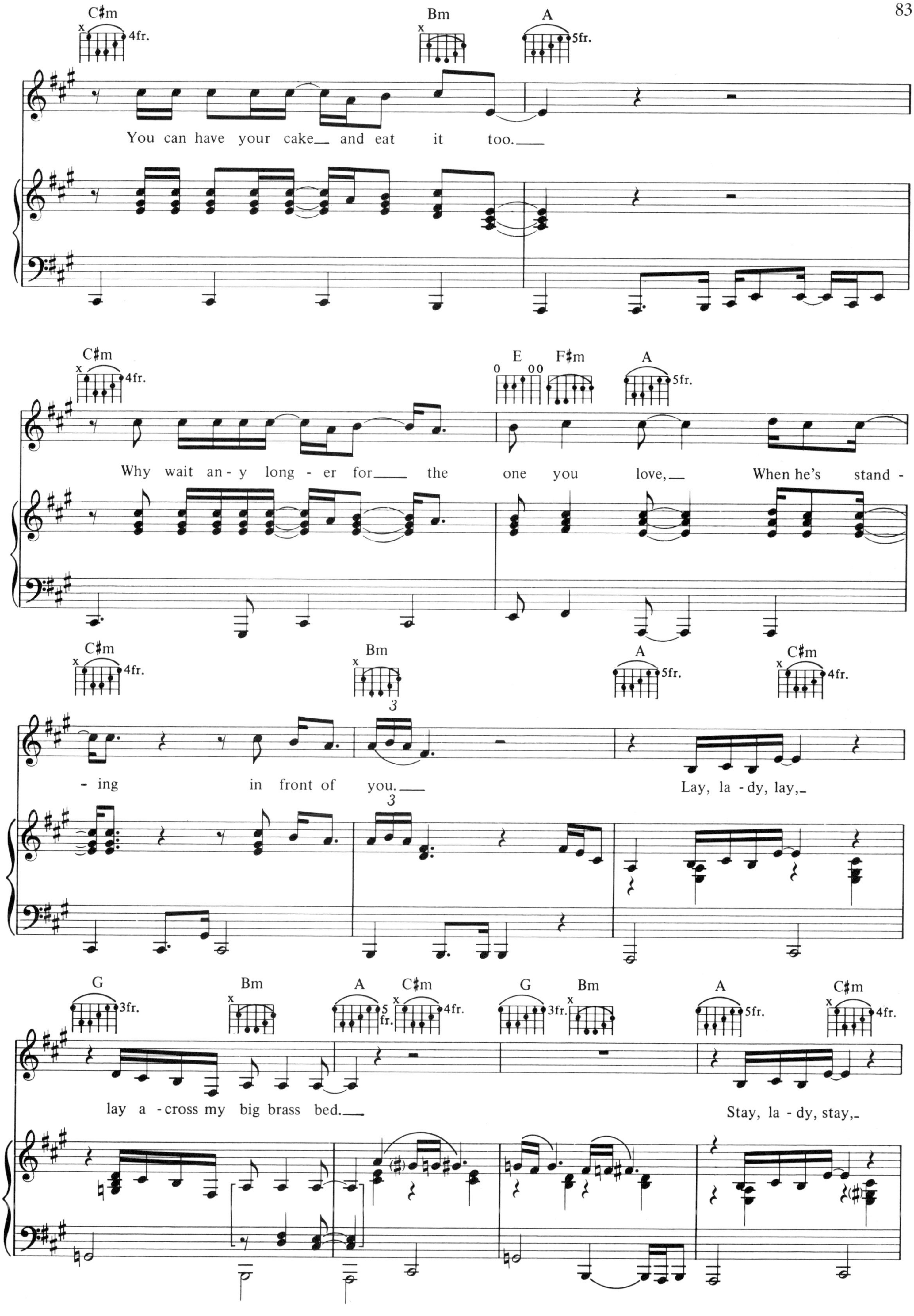
C♯m
4fr.
Bm
A
5fr.
You can have your cake and eat it too.
C♯m
4fr.
E
F♯m
A
5fr.
Why wait an - y long - er for the one you love, When he's stand -
C♯m
4fr.
Bm
3
A
5fr.
C♯m
4fr.
- ing in front of you.
Lay, la - dy, lay,
G
3fr.
Bm
A
5 fr.
C♯m
4fr.
G
3fr.
Bm
A
5fr.
C♯m
4fr.
lay a - cross my big brass bed.
Stay, la - dy, stay,

G
Bm
A
C♯m
G
Bm
3fr.
5fr.
4fr.
3fr.
stay while the night is still a - head.
E
F♯m
A
E
F♯m
5fr.
I long to see you in the morn-ing light,
I long to reach for you
A
C♯m/G♯
G
Bm/F♯
5fr.
4fr.
3fr.
in the night.
Stay, la - dy, stay,
stay while the night is still a - head.
A
C♯m
G
Bm
A
Bm
C♯m
D
A
5fr.
4fr.
3fr.
5fr.
4fr.
5fr.
5fr.

The Sound of Silence

Words and Music by Paul Simon

Dm
F
C
mains
with - in The
Sound
Of
Dm
Dm
C
Si - lence.
(2.) In rest - less dreams I walked a - lone
(3.) And in the nak - ed light I saw
mp (Melody)
Dm
F
nar - row streets of cob - ble - stone,
ten thou - sand peo - ple, may - be more.
'Neath the ha - lo of a
Peo - ple talk - ing with - out
B♭
F
B♭
F
street lamp,
speak - ing,
I turned my col - lar to the
peo - ple hear - ing with - out
cold and damp
lis - ten - ing

Bb
F
When my eyes were stabbed by the flash of a ne - on light that split the
Peo - ple writ - ing songs that voi - ces nev - er share and no one
Dm
F
C
Dm
night and touched The Sound Of Si - lence.
dare dis - turb The Sound Of Si - lence.
Dm
C
Dm
(4.) "Fools!" said I, "You do not know si - lence like a can - cer grows."
mf
F
Bb
F
"Hear my words that I might teach you, Take my arms that I might

B♭
F
reach you."
But my words like si - lent rain- drops
F
Dm
C
fell,
and ech- oed in the wells of
si - lence.
(5.) And the peo - ple bowed and prayed
to the ne - on god they made.
And the sign flashed out its
f

Bb
F
warn - ing.
In the words that it was form - ing,
And the signs said "The words of the proph - ets are writ - ten on the sub - way
walls and ten - e - ment halls"
And whis - per'd in The
Sounds Of Si - lence.
Dm
C
poco a poco dim.
mp
poco a poco ritard.
(Melody)
p
pp

Duncan

Words and Music by Paul Simon

D
Em
song, here's my song.
Em
D
2. My fath - er was a fish - er - man, my ma - ma was a fish - er - man's friend, And
G
A
D
I was born in the bore - dom and the chow - der, So
C
G
C
G
when I reached my prime, I left my home in the Mar - i - times,

C
G
D
Em
Head - ed down the turn - pike for New Eng - land, __ sweet New Eng - land.
C
G
C
G
C
Instrumental solo
G
Em
D
Em
Em
D
3. Holes in my con - fi - dence, _ holes in the knees of my jeans, I's

G A D C G
left with - out a pen - ny in my pock - et, Oo hoo hoo wee, I's a - bout
C G C G
des - ti - tut - ed as a kid could be, And I wished I wore a ring so I could
D Em
hock it, I'd like to hock it.
4. A
Em D
young girl in a park - ing lot was preach - in' to a crowd, sing - in'
5
5

G
A
D
sa - cred songs and read - ing from the Bi - ble, Well, I
C
G
C
G
told her I was lost, and she told me all a - bout the Pen - te - cost, And I
C
G
D
seen that girl as the road to my sur - vi -
Em
C
G
C
val.
Instrumental solo

G
C
G
Em
D
Em
Em
5. Just lat - er on the ver - y same night when I
D
G
A
crept to her tent with a flash - light, And my long years of in - no - cence
D
C
G
end - ed, Well, she took me to the woods, say - in',

C
G
C
G
"Here comes some - thin' and it feels so good!" And just like a dog I was be -
D
Em
friend - ed, I was be - friend - ed.
Em
D
6. Oh, oh, what a night, oh, what a gar - den of de - light, Ev - en
G
A
D
now that sweet mem - o - ry ling - ers, I was

C G C G

play - in' my gui - tar, ly - ing un - der - neath the stars, Just

C G D Em

thank - in' the Lord for my fin - gers, for my fin - gers.

Fade out

C G C G

C G Em D Em

Kathy's Song

Words and Music by Paul Simon

G Bm G C
Soft and warm con - tin - u - ing
I gaze be - yond the rain - drenched streets
They lie with you when you're a - sleep
Am Em D
Tap - ping on my roof and
To Eng - land where my heart
And kiss you when you start your
G C G G C G
walls.
lies.
day.
G C G
4. And a song I was writ - ing is left un - done
5. And so you see I have come to doubt
6. And as I watch the drops of rain

Am
Em
C
Bm7
I don't know why I spend my time
All that I once held as true
Weave their wear - y paths and die
G
Bm
G
C
writ - ing songs I can't be - lieve
I stand a - lone with - out be - liefs
I know that I am like the rain
Am
Em
D
G
C
With words that tear and strain to rhyme.
The on - ly truth I know is you.
There but for the grace of you go I.
G
G
C
1.2.
G
3.
G
C
G

Me And Julio Down By The Schoolyard

Words and Music by Paul Simon

No chord
D
It's a - gainst the law,
It was a - gainst the
G
law,
D
What the ma - ma saw,
G
It was a - gainst the law.
The
(In a)
G
ma - ma looked down and spit on the ground ev - 'ry time my name gets
cou - ple of days they come and take me a - way, but the press let the sto - ry

C
D
men - tioned,
The pa - pa said, "Oy, if I
leak,
And when the rad - i - cal priest come to
get that boy___ I'm gon - na stick him in the house of de - ten -
get me re - leased,___ we's all on the cov - er of News -
G
No chord
C
- tion."
- week.
Well, I'm on my way,___
G
C
I don't know where I'm go - in',___ I'm on my way,___

G
A
D
I'm tak - in' my time___ but I don't know where.___ Good - bye
C
F
G
Ro - - - sie, the Queen of Co - ro - na,
F
C
(E bass)
D
See you, Me And Ju - lio Down By The School - yard.__
G
C
G
D
G
F
See you, Me And Ju - lio

C
(E bass)
D
1. G
C
G
D
Down By The School - yard.
In a
2. G
C
G
D
G
F
See you, Me And Ju - lio
C
(E bass)
D
G
C
G
D
Down By The School - yard.
Fade out
G
C
G
D
Instrumental solo

Slip Slidin' Away

Words and Music by Paul Simon

C
D
C
C7
G
Db
Eb
Db
Db7
Ab
pas - sion for his wom - an like a thorn - y crown.
ver - y words she us - es to des - cribe her life.
ma - tion is un - a - vail - a - ble to the mor - tal man.
He said, "De - lor - es,
She said, "A good day
We work our jobs,
Em7
G
D
Fm7
Ab
Eb
I live in fear.
ain't got no rain."
col - lect our pay.
My love for you is so o - ver - pow-'ring I'm a - fraid
She said, "A bad day is when I lie in bed and think
Be - lieve we are glid - ing down the high - way when in fact
C
D
G
Db
Eb
Ab
To Coda
1.
2.
that I will dis - ap - pear.
of things that might have been.
we are slip slid - in' a - way.
Slip slid - in' a -
Slip slid - in' a -

G
Ab
Em
Fm
way. slip slid - in' a - way. You know the
D
Eb
C
Db
near-er your des - ti - na - tion the more you're slip slid - in' a - way.
F
Gb
And I know a fa - ther who had a son.
C7
Db7
He longed to tell him all the rea-sons for the things he'd done. He came a

G6
Ab6
Em7
Fm73
G
Ab
D
Eb
long way just to ex - plain.
He kissed his boy as he lay sleep-ing, then he
C
Db
D
Eb
G
Ab
turned a-round and head-ed home a - gain.
Slip slid - in' a - way,
Em
Fm
slip slid - in' a - way.
You know the near - er your des - ti - na - tion the more
you're slip slid - in' a - way.
F
Gb
C
Db

G
F
C
G
A♭
G♭
D♭
A♭
D. S. al Coda
God on - ly knows
Coda
G
A♭
Slip slid - in' a - way,
slip slid - in' a -
Em
Fm
G
A♭
D
E♭
way.
You know the near - er your des - ti - na - tion the more
C
D♭
D
E♭
G
A♭
you're slip slid - in' a - way.
Slip slid - in' a -

Em
G
D
Fm
A♭
E♭
way.
You know the near er your des - ti - na - tion the more
C
D
G
Em
D♭
E♭
A♭
Fm
you're slip slid - in' a - way.
Mm.
G
A♭
Mm,
mm, mm, mm, mm, mm, mm, mm, mm.
1. - 5.
Em
Fm
Mm.
6.
Em
Fm

Homeward Bound

Words and Music by Paul Simon

Dm
Bb
On a tour of one night stands my suit-case and gui-tar
And each town looks the same to me, the mov-ies and the fac-
But all my words come back to me in shades of me-di-oc-
C
in hand and ev-'ry stop is neat-ly planned for a
-tor-ies and ev-'ry strang-er's face I see re-
-ri-ty like emp-ti-ness in har-mon-ny I
G7
C
po-et and a one man band.
minds me that I long to be,
need some-one to com-fort me.
Chorus:
C
F
C
Home-ward Bound, I wish I was,

F
C
Home - ward Bound.
Home where my thought's
Dm C B♭ F C Dm C B♭ F C
es - cap - ing, Home where my mu - sic's play - ing, Home where my love
Dm C B♭ F G7 C
1.2. C
3. C Cmaj7
lies wait - ing si - lent - ly for me.
3. To -
C7 C F C
Si - lent - ly for me.

Morning Has Broken

Words by Eleanor Farjeon
Musical Arrangement by Cat Stevens

C
Em
Am
D7sus
D
ing, Black - bird has spok - en like the first
en, Like the first dew - fall on the first
G
C
F
bird. Praise for the sing - ing,
grass. Praise for the sweet - ness
C
Am
D
G
C
Praise for the morn - ing, Praise for them spring -
of the wet gar - den, Sprung in com - plete -
F
G7
C
F
ing fresh from the world.
ness where his feet pass.
mf

G
E
Am
1
G
C
G7sus
Am
2
F♯
Bm
G
D
A7
(D Bass)
D
rall.

a tempo
D
Em
A
G
3. Mine is the sun - light, Mine is the morn -
mp
D
F#m
Bm
E7
A
ing, Born of the one light E - den saw play.
D
G
D
Bm
Praise with e - la - tion, Praise ev-'ry morn -
E
A
D
G
A7
D
ing, God's re-cre - a - tion of the new day.
mf

G
A
F♯
Bm
G7
C
F
D.𝄋 al ⊕ Coda
C
Coda
Am
F♯
Bm
G
D
A7
D
rall.

Moonshadow

Words and Music by Cat Stevens

D F♯m Bm Em A
1. D
2. D
I won't have to work no more, and
I won't have to cry no more, yes
A7 D G A7 D
I'm be-in' fol-lowed by a moon shad-ow, moon shad-ow, moon shad-ow,
A7 D G A7 D
leap-in' and hop - in' on a moon shad-ow, moon shad-ow, moon shad-ow, and
G F♯m G D G F♯m
if I ev - er lose my legs, I won't moan and
if I ev - er lose my mouth, or my teeth

Em7
A7
G
F♯m
Em
F♯m
Em
A7
I won't beg, yes if I ev - er lose my legs, Oh if
north or south, yes if I ev - er lose my mouth, Oh if
D
F♯m
Bm
Em
A7
D
Em
A7
1.
2.
I won't have to walk any more and
I won't have to talk.
D
G
D
A7
D
E7
A
E
A
Did it take long to find me? I asked the faith - ful light.
f

E
A
E7
A
Did it take long to find me and are you gon-na stay the night. Oh
p
D
A7
D
G
A
D
I'm be-in' fol-lowed by a moon shad-ow, moon shad-ow, moon shad-ow,
A7
D
G
A7
D
leap-in' and hop-in' on a moon shad-ow, moon shad-ow, moon shad-ow,
G
A7
D
G
A7
D
moon shad-ow, moon shad-ow,
moon shad-ow, moon shad-ow.

Peace Train

Words and Music by Cat Stevens

C G C F C F
out on — the edge — of dark-ness — there rides — a peace train. Oh,
G Am F G F
peace train — take — this coun-try, come take — me home — a-gain. Now
C G C F C F
I've been — smil - in' late-ly — think-in' a-bout the good things — to come,
G Am F G F
and I — be-lieve — it could — be. Some-thing — good has be-gun. Oh,

C
G7
C
G7
C
F
C
F
peace train sound - in' loud-er, glide on the peace train.
F
G
Am
F
G
F
Come on the peace train.
C
G7
C
G7
C
F
C7
F
Peace train ho - ly roll-er, ev-'ry-one jump up on the peace train.
F
G
Am
F
G
F
To Coda
Come on now peace train.

C
G
C
F
C
F
Get your bags together go bring your good friends too. Because it's gettin' nearer it soon will be with you. Oh
F
G
Am
F
G
F
come and join the living it's not so far from you.
C
G
C
F
C
F
and it's gettin' nearer soon it will all be true. Oh
F
G
Am
F
G
F

C
G7
F
C7
G
Am
Peace Train sound - ing loud-er glide on _ the Peace Train OO
come on _ now Peace Train, Peace Train.
Now
I've been _ cry - in' late-ly _ think - in' a - bout the world as it is
3

F G Am F G F
why must _ we go ___ on hat - ing why can't _ we live in bliss. 'Cause
C G C F C F
out on _ the edge of dark - ness ___ there rides _ a Peace Train Oh
F G Am F G F
D.S. al Coda
Peace Train _ take ___ this coun - try come take _ me home ___ a - gain. Oh
Coda
F G Am F G Am F C
come on ___ Peace ___ Train yes it's _ the Peace Train!

Oh Very Young

Words and Music by Cat Stevens

D A D A A7
(C♯ Bass)
— fa - ding up to the sky___ and though you want him to last for - ev - er you know
D B E
he nev - er will,_ you know he nev - er will, and the pat - ches make the Good -
E7
(G♯ Bass)
A E A E
-bye hard - er still.
mf
f
A D E F♯m D E
Oh ve - ry young_ what will you leave_ us this time___ there'll nev - er
mf
A D E
be a bet - ter chance to change your mind___ and if you want this world to see a bet - ter day

A
D
A
will you car - ry the words of love with you will you ride
D
A
D
A
A7
(C♯ bass)
the great white bird in - to heav - en and though you want to last for - ev - er you know
D
B
E
you nev - er will you know you nev - er will, and the good - bye makes the jour -
E7
(G♯ Bass)
A
E
A
E
A
ney hard - er still
D
E
D
E
A
D
E

A
D
A
D
will you car - ry the words_ of love_ with you will you ride
A
A7
(C♯ Bass)
D
B
E
A
(C♯ Bass)
Bm
E
Oh
A
E
A
E
A
Oh ve - ry young
D
E
F♯m
D
E
E7
(G♯ Bass)
A
what will you leave us this time you're on - ly dan - cing on this earth for a short
p
D
E
A
while Oh ve - ry young what will you leave us this time
mf
Ritard.

Hard Headed Woman

Words and Music by Cat Stevens

Dm G C Cm F
I'm look-ing for a hard headed wom-an One who'll make me do my
Dm Am B♭ G C F
to Coda
best. And if I find my hard head-ed wom - an.
B♭ C F Am
I know the rest of my life will be blessed, yes, yes, yes.
Dm G C Cm F
I know a lot of fan - cy danc - ers Peo-ple who can glide you on a

Dm
Am
F
B♭
F
B♭
F
C
floor, They move so smooth but have no ans-wers
Gm
C
F
Am
when you ask why'd you come here for?
(spoken)
Why?
(I don't know)
Am
D
Am
I know man-y fine feath-ered friends but their
They know man-y sure fired ways to find
D
F
E
friend-li-ness de-pends on how you do.
out the one who pays and how you do.

A
Dm
G
C
I'm look- ing for a hard head-ed wom - an.
Cm
F
Dm
Am
F
B♭
F
B♭
F
one who will make me feel so good.
And if I find my hard head-ed
C
Gm
C
F
Am
D.S. al Coda
wom-an
I know my life will be as it should, yes yes, yes.
Coda
Dm
G
Dm
G
Dm
G
Dm

Another Saturday Night

Words and Music by Sam Cooke

F
F7
B♭
F
F7
seen a lot of girls since then, if I could meet 'em I could get 'em but as
sis-ter who looked just fine in-stead of be-in' my de-liv-'rance she
he don't know his way a-round if I don't find me a hon-ey to
B♭
F
C
F
C
1.
yet I have-n't met 'em that's how I'm in the state I'm in. Oh an-oth-er
had a strange re-sem-blance to a cat named Frank-en-stein.
help me spend my mon-ey I'm gon-na have to blow this town.
F
C
2.
D.S. 𝄋 al ⊕ Coda
Ooh la A-noth-er
Oh no A-noth-er
⊕ Coda
1.
D.S.
2.
(to instrumental)
A-noth-er

G
C
G
Sat - ur - day night - and I ain't got no - bod - y, I got some mon - ey 'cause I
D
G
C
just got paid; how I wish I had some - one to talk to.
G
D
G
D
G
D
I'm in an aw - ful, ooh, I'm in an aw - ful way, he's in an aw - ful way,
G
D
G
D
G
D
G
I'm in an aw - ful way, I'm in an aw - ful way, He's in an aw - ful way.

Wild World

Words and Music by Cat Stevens

F
Dm
E
G7
but then a lot of nice things turn bad out there.
but just re-mem-ber there's a lot of bad and be-ware.
C
G
F
G
F
Oh ba-by, ba - by it's a WILD WORLD.
It's hard to get by just up-on a
C
C
G
F
smile.
Oh, ba-by, ba - by it's a WILD WORLD
G
F
to Coda
1.
C
Dm
E
I'll al-ways re-mem - ber you like a child, girl.

C
Dm
E
Am
D7
G
Cmaj7
2.
child, girl.
F
Dm7
Baby I love you, But if you want to leave take good
care, hope you make a lot of nice friends out there. But just re-mem-ber there's a lot of bad
G7
D.S. al
and be-ware
CODA
child, girl.